Animal Yoga

RAVETTE PUBLISHING

First published by Ravette Publishing 2015

Ravette Publishing Limited
PO Box 876
Horsham
West Sussex RH12 9GH

ISBN: 978-1-84161-390-1

Less is often more

You're only as young as your spine is flexible

Don't take yourself too seriously, nobody else does

Life is full of risks

Sometimes
I feel as
if life has
passed me
by

If it's worth
doing,
it's worth
overdoing

Appreciate your body and its marvels

I'm my
own pig

I never know what's going on!

Every now
and then I
feel like my
existence is
justified

I can't stand all this responsibility

Born to be free

The best is yet to come!

Sometimes I feel like I want to run away from everything

Learn something new every day

Other titles available in this series ...

	ISBN	Price
Yoga Dogs - Get In Touch With Your Inner Pup	978-1-84161-357-4	£4.99
Yoga Cats - The Purrfect Workout	978-1-84161-356-7	£4.99
Yoga Puppies - The Ruff Guide to Yoga	978-1-84161-363-5	£4.99
Yoga Kittens - Take Life One Pose At A Time	978-1-84161-362-8	£4.99
Yoga Babies	978-1-84161-377-2	£4.99
Cow Yoga	978-1-84161-389-5	£5.99

How to order   Please send a cheque/postal order in £ sterling, made payable to 'Ravette Publishing' for the cover price of the book/s and allow the following for post & packaging ...

UK & BFPO	70p for the first book & 40p per book thereafter
Europe and Eire	£1.30 for the first book & 70p per book thereafter
Rest of the world	£2.20 for the first book & £1.10 per book thereafter

RAVETTE PUBLISHING LTD
PO Box 876, Horsham, West Sussex RH12 9GH
Tel: 01403 711443   Fax: 01403 711554   Email: info@ravettepub.co.uk
www.ravettepublishing.tel

Prices and availability are subject to change without prior notice.